Living Our United Methodist Beliefs

Living Our United Methodist Beliefs

GEORGE HOVANESS DONIGIAN

DISCIPLESHIP
RESOURCES

At the time of publication all websites referenced in this book were valid. However, due to the fluid nature of the Internet some addresses may have changed, or the content may no longer be relevant.

Library of Congress Control Number: 2014931629

ISBNs
Print: 978-0-88177-715-4
Mobi: 978-0-88177-716-1
Epub: 978-0-88177-717-8

DR 715

Contents

Preface

Thoughts on Teaching and Learning

Each of us has a personal and unique learning style. It may be similar to that of others, but if we are able to use a learning style tailored to the way our brain recognizes, stores, and processes information, learning becomes easy and fun, and information is more effectively retained. Think of how you prefer to learn. Perhaps you are a reader. Maybe you learn more easily and efficiently by listening to music, to other sounds, or to voice. Perhaps you learn best in a "hands-on" manner. If the teaching method suits your learning style, you can process and adapt any information quickly. Addressing the educational needs of all students during a session may require you to modify your presentation style.

While lecture alone is the least effective means of presenting material, group activity is one of the most effective. Relational activities in small groups, or sometimes in the larger class context, associate students with different learning styles and thereby offer a way for the teacher to expose students to multiple avenues of learning. Although some sessions will lend themselves to one or more specific learning styles, the instructor can use a combination to address the needs of students. As teachers, we need to be creative.

Articles and guidelines concerning multiple intelligences refer to the research of Howard Gardner, or the "eight ways of learning." These disciplines can be loosely grouped into three categories or styles: auditory, visual, or tactile (also known as kinesthetic, as it can involve any form of participatory motion or perceived movement). Here are some activity suggestions:

Auditory

Class discussion
Show-and-tell
Creative rhythms and raps
Debate
Paraphrase or description
Music, songs, or rhymes
Poetry, storytelling, and reading

Word games
Seminars

Visual

Charts and graphs
Time lines and diagrams
Cartoons and bulletin boards
Photographs and video
Posters
Journal writing
Montages, collages, and collections

Tactile

Games and simulations
Puppets
Sculpting
Drama, dance, and role-playing
Singing
Construction
Experiments
Origami and jigsaw puzzles

Introduction

When we consider the figure of John Wesley, most often we think of the practical theologian of the eighteenth century. We think of Wesley preaching and teaching around Great Britain, organizing societies, and seeking to spread scriptural holiness throughout the land. Such pictures of Wesley fail to help us see the creative genius of Wesley in responding to the needs of the culture surrounding him.

What is most important about this is that our own cultural problems mirror those of Wesley's epoch. As in our time, so in Wesley's time obstacles and barriers grew more considerably between economic and social classes. The upper class of Wesley's era did little in relation to the poor; those in the Wesleyan societies, who were in a class between England's wealthy and impoverished, related to both rich and poor. Wesleyans of the eighteenth century visited those in debtor's prisons and in mental institutions. By such visits, they helped make visible the caring love of God. In an era in which health care was rare, Wesley wrote *Primitive Physic: An Easy and Natural Method of Curing Most Diseases* as a way to offer rudimentary medical and health education. For more information on such parallels, see *John Wesley for the 21st Century*, by John O. Gooch (Discipleship Resources, 2006).

Before addressing the social needs as part of his effort to reform the nation, Wesley first began to go to the people. We know about Wesley's field preaching at coal mines and other gathering points. What we fail to remember is that the Church of England did nothing to address these people. The eighteenth-century Anglican Church focused primarily on upper-class patrons, and the churches were somewhat empty for worship. That moves us to consider a significant parallel with our own era. For many and different reasons, people are turned off by church. A majority of churches have too many empty seats for worship. To do as Wesley did means that we should seek creative and new venues for the proclamation of the gospel. Perhaps this means renting a nightclub for an evening of praise and worship or perhaps it means Bible study groups at the neighborhood coffee house. Perhaps it means offering words of grace on a television commercial during a sports telecast. As we approach the study of our United Methodist heritage, I hope that you and your congregation will learn to ask a basic question: What would John Wesley do?

To the Course Leader

A Note on Wesleyan Teaching

John and Charles Wesley taught their understandings of Christian doctrine through hymns. Methodists sang their theology. That remains true to this day, though we sometimes neglect to make overt and direct connections between the hymns we sing and the doctrines we teach and preach. You will find that each session of this study relies on Wesleyan hymnody to teach, guide, and inspire. Please do not short-circuit this approach by skipping the selected hymns. If you do not know the hymns yourself, find a musician who can teach them to you and to the class.

If John Wesley were to teach this course, he would read completely through the leader's guide before tackling the sessions. I trust that you will give yourself time to read the entire leader's guide and the related textbooks. Your experience and that of your participants will be much more fulfilling if you do.

You will see that each session has outcome goals listed. The session plans will enhance the desired learning outcomes. For this study, participants will gain a relatively broad and deep perspective on United Methodist heritage and the ways that this heritage can influence our work in the present and future. The outcome goals are listed in the appendix and may be printed and given to the participants at the beginning of the course.

The course as outlined takes ten hours. It may be taught on a weekend, in five two-hour sessions spread out over a five-week period, or on consecutive nights. The course is designed to be used in conferences or district lay servant training events, with a cluster of churches, or in a single congregation.

Because there are assignments that will require outside work, this course may best be conducted in five separate sessions. If teaching this course in a weekend format, you will need to provide assignments to the participants before the sessions begin.

This course is designed to encourage and facilitate a formative experience for course participants. As the leader, you undoubtedly have your own expectations for this course; however, there are some guidelines you will want to keep in mind. First, have an attitude for learning and a desire to learn from others. Even as leaders, we are learners. No one person has all the answers, holds all the truth, or has all the knowledge.

Second, even though you are the leader, do not talk too much. No one person should monopolize the group discussion. Everyone is encouraged to share ideas. A good group session is like an orchestra; each instrument serves the whole and adds to the overall performance.

Finally, be a good steward of time. Be respectful of the class time. Try to start and end on time. The old adage that it is better to end too soon than too late applies to healthy class sessions. It is better to leave wanting more than to leave feeling overloaded!

In the best sense of God's grace, remember that we go forward—forward in the sanctifying and perfecting love of God!

General Course Goals

By the end of the course each participant will:

1. Discover the place of doctrine in relation to the missional movement known as Methodism
2. Develop an understanding of Wesleyan theology and its influence on the practical structure and disciplines for the first Methodists
3. Acquire knowledge of Methodist history and the formation of other Methodist denominations
4. Explore the Wesleyan understanding of grace and how it became key to the movement
5. Describe and discuss the means of grace and how these disciplines lead to holiness of heart and life

Resources

Participants will read two basic texts:

Living Our Beliefs: The United Methodist Way by Kenneth L. Carder (Discipleship Resources, 2009)

A Brief History of The United Methodist Church (available from Amazon.com)

These texts will be supplemented by information and readings from *The Story of American Methodism* by Frederick A. Norwood (Abingdon, 1974), *How Great a Flame!* by James C. Logan (Discipleship Resources, 2005), *A Blueprint for Discipleship* by Kevin Watson (Discipleship Resources, 2009), and *Mainline or Methodist?* by Scott Kisker (Discipleship Resources, 2008).

Other books you will need are listed here:

Copies of *The United Methodist Hymnal* for all participants

The current edition of *The Book of Discipline of The United Methodist Church*

The United Methodist Book of Worship

You will also need the following:

Copies of the quiz in the appendix to distribute to each participant

Newsprint and markers or chalkboard and chalk

Musical accompaniment for singing, if possible

Copies of the Covenant Renewal Service (no. 288 in *The United Methodist Book of Worship*)

Participants are expected to bring some method of taking notes to class. Paper and ink or a digital tool will work.

Opening and closing worship information for sessions 2-4 and opening worship for session 5 are listed in the appendix. You may want to include the participants as leaders in these opening or closing worship times. Closing worship should be led by you with participation by class members.

Assignments are also listed in the appendix and may be photocopied and distributed to participants before the sessions start.

Session One

"And Can It Be that I Should Gain"

Note to the course leader: Before the first session, make sure each participant has a copy of the two basic books for the course—*Living Our Beliefs: The United Methodist Way* by Kenneth L. Carder and *A Brief History of The United Methodist Church*. Check the meeting area to be sure it is comfortably arranged and stocked with the following supplies: copies of *The United Methodist Hymnal*, newsprint or large sheets of blank white paper, markers, pencils, and/or pens. Make enough copies of the assessment test, "What do you know about United Methodist heritage?" (appendix) so that each participant will have a copy. You will need a computer, Internet connection, projector, and a screen to show the suggested video.

LEARNING GOAL

At the end of this session, participants will be able to articulate an overview of the life and ministry of John Wesley. They will gain an awareness of the place of doctrine in the missional movement known as Methodism. They will begin to see the history of Methodism by beginning a Wesley family tree.

OPENING WORSHIP (15 minutes)

Introduce yourself and allow participants to introduce themselves. After the introductions, sing "And Can It Be that I Should Gain" (*UMH*, no. 363). Use the following information to introduce the hymn, which Charles Wesley wrote after his conversion experience in May 1738: Like his brother John, Charles Wesley struggled to know the love of God and the assurance of forgiveness for himself. In May 1738, Charles recorded the following entries in his journal:

> Wed., May 17th. I experienced the power of Christ rescuing me in temptation. Today I first saw Luther on the Galatians, which Mr. Holland had accidentally lit upon. . . .

> Sat., May 20th. I waked much disappointed, and continued all day in great dejection, which the sacrament did not in the least abate. Nevertheless God would not suffer me to doubt the truth of his promises.
>
> [Sunday] May 21, 1738. I now found myself at peace with God, and rejoiced in hope of loving Christ. My temper for the rest of the day was, mistrust of my own great, but before unknown, weakness. I saw that by faith I stood; by the continual support of faith, which kept me from falling, though of myself I am ever sinking into sin. I went to bed still sensible of my own weakness, (I humbly hope to be more and more so,) yet confident of Christ's protection.
>
> [Wednesday] May 24, 1738. At midnight I gave myself up to Christ: assured I was safe, sleeping or waking. I had continued experience of his power to overcome all temptation; and confessed, with joy and surprise, that he was able to do exceedingly abundantly for me, above what I can ask or think.
>
> Both Wesley brothers experienced an assurance of grace as a result of their diligent search and struggle. From that experience, Charles wrote a hymn that he titled "Free Grace," which we know as "And Can It Be that I Should Gain." Let us sing the hymn (or if no musical accompaniment is available, read aloud the words together).

After singing "And Can It Be that I should Gain," ask the group how the hymn connects with their own experience of God's grace. Following a brief time of exchanging stories, invite the group to join in an opening prayer. You may pray the following prayer: Loving God, all-wise and wonderful, to you we give thanks for the beauty of this day and the witness of history. Encourage us to learn about our heritage and to grow in our sense of mission for this time in the life of the world. We join our prayers now together with the words Jesus taught, saying; Our Father, who art in heaven. . . .

TAKE A TEST (15 minutes)

Distribute copies of the assessment test and allow participants ten minutes to complete it. When everyone has completed the assessment, ask participants if any of the questions surprised them. Take time to go over the answers and offer participants an opportunity to ask questions about the test or to express any frustrations or surprises that occurred to them.

VIDEO PRESENTATION (10 minutes)

Show the following video to help set the context of Methodism in the United States: <http://www.youtube.com/watch?v=G_BGLMk37Xs&feature=player_embedded>

THE BASIC STORY OF JOHN WESLEY (20 minutes)

Use the following highlights to tell participants about the life of John Wesley. (You may wish to supplement this information with references to chapter 1 in *The Story of American Methodism* by Frederick A. Norwood.)

John Wesley was born in 1703, the fifteenth child of nineteen children in the family of the Reverend Samuel and Susanna Wesley. Samuel Wesley was a priest in the Church of England and rector of the church in Epworth. Susanna managed the household and educated her children in languages, mathematics, and other fields of education. When he was eleven, John went to a public school (in reality, a private school). From there he followed in his father's educational footsteps and went to Oxford University. Wesley was ordained a priest in the Church of England in 1728.

Throughout this time of young adulthood, both John and Charles Wesley struggled with questions of faith. They asked whether God truly forgave them. They participated in small-group Bible study at the university—to the point that other people at Oxford referred to the Wesleys and their friends with the derogatory names of "the Holy Club," "Bible moths," and "Methodists."

Wesley continued his studies and tried some fields of endeavor. In 1735, at the request of Governor Oglethorpe, John and Charles Wesley sailed for Savannah, Georgia. Their intent was to minister to the Anglican parish in Savannah and to engage in mission work with Native Americans. While crossing the Atlantic, the ship encountered several storms. Fearing for his life, John felt a deep terror. He encountered Moravian Christians on the ship who did not share his anxiety or terror. During a storm, the Moravians calmly sang hymns. In response to Wesley's questions concerning the calm of the Moravians, their leader, August Spangenberg, responded by speaking of their trust in God. He asked Wesley about his own experience of God and whether he had an assurance of salvation within himself. Wesley did not speak with confidence of that assurance.

The mission to Georgia was a disaster for the Wesley brothers. Their mission work with Native Americans was unsuccessful, and Wesley's attitude toward church differed greatly from those of the colonists in Georgia. (An aside about the state of Georgia: A number of British Parliamentarians were concerned about the growing number of people in debtor's prison. After some lobbying and the British government's recognition of a need to provide a buffer between its South Carolina colony and the Spanish territory in Florida, the British government agreed to send a number of prisoners to establish a "Province of Georgia," which was named after King George II. In 1733, approximately one hundred settlers arrived at what would become Savannah. Under the direction of James Oglethorpe, the original design of Savannah was laid out and the rudimentary colony began to grow.)

Note to the course leader: At this interval, you may wish to explain the romantic interest with Sophia Hopkey and the end of that story.

With the failure of their work in Georgia, John and Charles Wesley returned to England where they plunged again into the Holy Club routine. John met Peter Boehler, another Moravian, who was waiting for permission to go to Georgia. Their conversations dealt with Wesley's doubt and anxiety concerning salvation. On May 24, 1738, the pivotal spiritual experience for John Wesley occurred. He recorded the following in his journal on May 24, 1738:

> In the evening I went very unwillingly to a society in Aldersgate Street, where one was reading Luther's preface to the Epistle to the Romans. About a quarter before nine, while he was describing the change which God works in the heart through faith in Christ, I felt my heart strangely warmed. I felt I did trust in Christ, Christ alone, for salvation; and an assurance was given me that He had taken away my sins, even mine, and saved me from the law of sin and death.
>
> I began to pray with all my might for those who had in a more especial manner despitefully used me and persecuted me. I then testified openly to all there what I now first felt in my heart. But it was not long before the enemy suggested, "This cannot be faith; for where is thy joy?" Then was I taught that peace and victory over sin are essential to faith in the Captain of our salvation; but that, as to the transports of joy that usually attend the beginning of it, especially in those who have mourned deeply, God sometimes giveth, sometimes withholdeth, them according to the counsels of His own will.
>
> After my return home, I was much buffeted with temptations, but I cried out, and they fled away. They returned again and again. I as often lifted up my eyes, and He "sent me help from his holy place." And herein I found the difference between this and my former state chiefly consisted. I was striving, yea, fighting with all my might under the law, as well as under grace. But then I was sometimes, if not often, conquered; now, I was always conqueror.

You may wish to remind participants of the experience of Charles Wesley that led to the writing of the hymn "Free Grace" or "And Can It Be that I Should Gain."

From that point, John Wesley understood himself as a new creation in Christ. The old had indeed passed away, and God was doing something new through him. After the Aldersgate experience, Wesley went to Herrnhut, the Moravian headquarters in Germany, where he studied and learned. He returned to England later in 1738. He created rules of discipline for the small groups known as bands. He published a collection of hymns and taught the religious societies around London.

Wesley was excluded from most churches within the Anglican communion in England. In the same way, the evangelist George Whitefield was also excluded. Whitefield began to preach outdoors, a surprising development then. In 1739, Wesley preached his first outdoor sermon with Whitefield. Though he did not care to preach away from church sanctuaries, Wesley preached wherever he could. Until his death, Wesley preached in fields, chapels, cottages, market crosses, and sometimes, when invited, in churches.

Ask what questions participants have concerning Wesley. Write the questions on the chalkboard or newsprint. You will find ways to deal with these questions during this course.

SING A HYMN (5 minutes)

Close the first half of this session by reading aloud John Wesley's Directions for Singing on page vii of *The United Methodist Hymnal* and singing the first and last stanzas of "And Can It Be that I Should Gain" (*UMH*, no. 363).

BREAK (10 minutes)

Allow participants time to stretch.

SING A HYMN (5 minutes)

Reconvene and invite the class to join together in singing "Come, Sinners, to the Gospel Feast" (*UMH*, no. 339). After singing, ask participants how Charles Wesley speaks the message of grace through the hymn.

CONVERSATION ON METHODIST DOCTRINE (20 minutes)

Ask for a volunteer to read aloud slowly the list of shared beliefs on page 16 of *Living Our Beliefs: The United Methodist Way* by Kenneth L. Carder. After a brief period of silence, ask for a second volunteer to read aloud the same list. After the second reading, ask participants how they feel about this list. Then ask the following question: "Are there any surprises here? Were you aware of these theological affirmations? Did anything surprise you or stand out for you?" Use the following highlights to discuss Carder's assertions in the chapter:

> Carder points to a lack of denominational loyalty and attributes this loss to several factors. He points to United Methodist churches that avoid identifying themselves with United Methodism by naming themselves "Fellowship Chapel" or "Community Church." Some of the factors Carder identifies include religious pluralism and movement from one church to another, denominational dysfunction, and theological controversies. He points out that the church needs to recover its identity and describes a form of cultural amnesia. Carder is convinced that as we learn and understand our theological doctrine, we will also gain new identity as a church.
>
> Carder writes about the Wesleyan movement as one of mission and reform. He notes that John Wesley described the mission of Methodism as "to reform the nation, particularly the Church, and to spread scriptural holiness over the land." Invite participants to respond to Wesley's summary statement.

> Carder also writes about the need for revival. He writes about the goal of plain doctrine as a doorway into the knowledge and love of God. He notes that the transformation of the world is God's great concern, not the statistical growth of the institutional church. Carder reminds us that the church is an instrument of God's mission. What would revival mean if we consider such revival as more clearly establishing the reign of God?

Invite conversation after the summary by using Carder's reflection questions on page 21.

WESLEY FAMILY TREE (12-15 minutes)

Distribute to each participant a sheet of newsprint, pencils, pens, or markers. Invite the class to begin work on a family tree that will trace their congregation's roots back to John Wesley. Work on the vertical scale of the paper. Begin with John and Charles Wesley at the top center and draw a vertical line to the bottom of the paper. Include the birth and death dates for the Wesley brothers. About two inches down from the Wesley brothers, draw two rectangles—one for Francis Asbury and the other for Thomas Coke.

Tell participants that they will continue work on this project and will include other members of the Wesleyan family and that the completed family tree will include the name of the particular bishop when their congregation began. For each entry on the Wesley family tree, they will draw a box in a line below the Wesleys. Each box should include name, important dates, and relevant information.

Ask participants to find out when their church was chartered and learn the names of the first pastor, district superintendent (or presiding elder), and bishop.

CLOSING WORSHIP (5 minutes)

Invite participants to express any prayer requests—joys and concerns—and ask them to join together in prayer. Lead a brief time of prayer and invite participants to join in praying together the Lord's Prayer. After the time of prayer, sing stanzas 3 and 4 of "Come, Sinners, to the Gospel Feast" (*UMH*, no. 339).

ASSIGNMENT FOR THE NEXT SESSION

Ask participants to read chapters 2 and 3 of *Living Our Beliefs: The United Methodist Way* in preparation for the next session. Remind the class of their assignment to learn more about the start of their particular congregation and to bring their Wesley family trees to the next session.

Session Two

In Whom We Live

Note to the course leader: Prepare the room. For this session you will need paper and pencils or pens for participants and everyone should bring their copy of *Living Our Beliefs: The United Methodist Way.*

LEARNING GOAL

Participants will gain a deeper sense of John Wesley's theological understanding of God and how that understanding inspired Wesley to create the practical structure and disciplines for the first Methodists.

OPENING WORSHIP (10 minutes)

Invite the class to sing "Maker, in Whom We Live" (*UMH*, no. 88). After singing the hymn, tell the group that John and Charles Wesley taught through their hymns. Ask the class what this hymn teaches about God. You may invite participants to list the specific theological terms in the hymn. Allow time for discussion. Then pray together, thanking God for the class time and for the participants. Invite the presence of the Holy Spirit to sustain and guide the class session.

REVIEW THE PREVIOUS SESSION (15 minutes)

Ask participants to form groups of three to review the content of session 1. Allow the groups ten minutes for this conversation. Then ask the entire class to respond to the following question:
How did the hymns sung in session 1 speak to your spiritual journey? What surprised you about the first session?

LEARN ABOUT A METHODIST ESSENTIAL (30 minutes)

Participants will need paper and a pen or pencil. Say to participants: "The assessment test included this assertion: Bortnagle Kudzu said, 'The only difference between the Methodist church and the Baptists down the street is that they sing different hymns.' In other places, similar comparisons were made between Methodists and other churches. One implication of such a generalized statement is that Methodists have no doctrinal expectations or doctrinal standards. Let's begin to look at our understanding of doctrine."

Ask participants to turn to chapter 2 in *Living Our Beliefs: The United Methodist Way*, which is properly titled "God Versus Idols." Invite participants to form groups of three to review the highlights of the chapter. Allow five minutes for this exercise. Participants should remain in groups of threes after this exercise is completed. After this period of review, ask for a volunteer to read aloud the section titled "Practical Divinity" on page 27.

Ask the groups to list their ideas of holy living. These may be attributes such as generosity or service to others or they may be actions such as prayer and daily Bible reading. Invite volunteers to share their lists and write these on the chalkboard or on newsprint. Then invite the group to try to arrange these ideas in terms of "must-have" priorities. You may also ask the group to narrow down the list to five basic items, asking why these are priorities. In essence, you are asking the participants to describe what matters the most to them.

Following this exercise, ask the group to think about what shapes their beliefs and their holy living. Carder lists several factors that cause conflict. These include success, consumerism, and hedonism. Invite the groups to take five to seven minutes for conversation about these sections of chapter 2. Allow participants to share any significant insights or points of agreement or disagreement with Carder's statements.

Two questions on page 36 of Carder's book concern the ways our beliefs are shaped. Remaining in groups of three, invite half of the groups to join in conversation on question 1 and the other half of the groups to discuss question 3. After ten minutes, ask volunteers to share their insights concerning each question.

BREAK (10 minutes)

Allow participants time to stretch.

SING A HYMN (5 minutes)

Reconvene and invite the class to join together in singing "Come, Sinners, to the Gospel Feast" (*UMH*, no. 339). After singing, ask participants what theological concerns and emphases Charles Wesley writes about in the hymn.

EXPLORE WESLEYAN BELIEFS ABOUT GOD (30 minutes)

Ask participants to turn to "I'll Praise My Maker While I've Breath" (*UMH*, no. 60) and read the hymn aloud together. Ask participants to name what this hymn tells them about God. Allow ten to twelve minutes for the conversation.

Tell participants that a basic Wesleyan theological belief concerns the Trinity. Invite a volunteer to read aloud the first two paragraphs in the section titled "The God We Know as Trinity" on page 41 of *Living Our Beliefs: The United Methodist Way*. Then invite another volunteer to read aloud the second paragraph and hymn stanzas on page 42. Invite a third volunteer to read aloud the first two paragraphs on page 44 concerning the Holy Spirit. Ask participants to gather in groups of three to discuss these basic statements concerning the parts of the Trinitarian understanding of God. After a suitable interval, ask the groups to share their sense of the Trinity, especially as their theological understanding relates to the following question from *Living Our Beliefs: The United Methodist Way*, "What difference does your faith in the Triune God make in how you live?" (page 49).

CONTINUE THE WESLEY FAMILY TREE (10-15 minutes)

Invite participants to join in groups organized around their church's age: under 20 years, 21-50 years, 51-100 years, 101-150 years, 151-200 years, and 201+ years. Ask the groups to share together any information they learned about the founding pastor and the bishop who presided over the annual conference when their church was formed. Invite participants to tell one another about their research concerning their congregation's history. Make certain to ask the groups to identify the branch of The United Methodist Church in which their congregation is rooted.

CLOSING WORSHIP (5 minutes)

Invite participants to join in an affirmation of the Triune God by reciting the Apostles' Creed. Then ask them to express any prayer requests—joys and concerns—and join together in prayer. Lead a brief time of prayer and invite participants to join in praying together the Lord's Prayer.

ASSIGNMENT FOR THE NEXT SESSION

Ask participants to read chapters 4 and 5 of *Living Our Beliefs: The United Methodist Way* in preparation for the next session. Remind them of their assignment to learn more about the start of their particular congregation and to bring their Wesley family trees to the next session. Ask participants if anyone plays the flute or bassoon. If someone plays one of these instruments, ask if he or she would be willing to accompany a hymn during one of the next sessions.

Session Three

Mission, Ministry, and Innovation

Note to the course leader: Prepare the room. For this session participants will need their copy of *Living Our Beliefs: The United Methodist Way* and you will need to bring copies of *The United Methodist Hymnal* for everyone.

LEARNING GOAL

At the end of this session participants will be able to identify many of the innovations that came through John Wesley and the early Methodist movement. They will also learn about the church's history and the formation of other Methodist denominations.

OPENING WORSHIP (10 minutes)

Invite the class to sing "O Come and Dwell in Me" (*UMH*, no. 388). After singing the hymn, tell the group that John and Charles Wesley taught through their hymns. Ask the group to name what they proclaim when they sing "O Come and Dwell in Me." Then pray together, thanking God for the class time and for the participants.

WESLEYAN INNOVATION (40 minutes)

Ask participants what they would identify as innovations that came from the Wesley brothers and the early Methodist movement. Here are some examples to include:

Field preaching: In Wesley's England, the country was divided into parishes and pastoral responsibility within each parish went to the duly designated Anglican priest. Parish boundaries were respected—until John Wesley began to proclaim, "The world is my parish."

Preaching to the people wherever the people were: To preach at 5 a.m. was innovative!

Field music: Methodists sang and invited others to join in the singing of hymns. In the field preaching, hymns were generally accompanied by either the flute or the bassoon. (Hauling around a harpsichord or clavichord or the relatively new invention (around 1700)—the piano—is not recommended for field preaching.)

Lay preaching: Wesley taught, examined, and appointed laity as local preachers to lead worship and preach. They could not administer the sacraments. These lay preachers were trusted by Wesley to further the mission of the movement.

Women's leadership: Women were class leaders and responsible for societies and bands. Unlike other eighteenth-century church experiences and expectations, Methodist women visited the sick and those in prison, taught children, and engaged in acts of mission and service.

The society: Each society included individuals in a given area who were members of the Methodist classes in that area. Societies might number in the hundreds. The society was similar to the gathering of Sunday school classes. People came to the society to sing hymns and pray, to hear scripture read and the Bible preached.

The class meeting: The class meeting was the most basic part of Methodism. Twelve to twenty members were in each class of mixed ages and social status. Classes included men and women. Classes met weekly (a weeknight) under the direction of a lay member known as the class leader. Classes were organized to guide members in holy living. Class leaders asked each person in the class one basic question: "How is it with your soul?" Class members were given tickets that allowed them to participate in society gatherings. All Methodists were expected to participate in class meetings and society gatherings.

The select band: This was a more intense experience than the class meeting. Participation in the band or select band was not mandatory. About six people participated in a band meeting. The bands were segregated by sex. The following questions were asked of each participant in the bands:

> What known sins have you committed since our last meeting?
> What temptations have you met with?
> How were you delivered?
> What have you thought, said, or done, of which you doubt whether it be sin or not?
> Have you nothing you desire to keep secret? (This question was optional.)

Use this information to give participants an overview of Wesley's innovations. Make sure everyone understands the relationship of society, class, and band. You may also explain that the early British Methodists remained a part of the Church of England and that their participation in Methodist class meetings and societies came in addition to their participation in Anglican services of worship. Be certain that participants understand that the early structure of Methodism was intended as a means for each Methodist to live a holy life or to live with holiness of heart. Note also that these innovations grew from the Wesleyan understanding of the mission to "spread scriptural holiness and to reform the nation."

BREAK (10 minutes)

Allow participants time to stretch.

SING A HYMN (5 minutes)

Sing "A Charge to Keep I Have" (*UMH*, no. 413). If someone can accompany the hymn with a flute or bassoon or other solitary instrument, do so. After singing the hymn, ask participants how this hymn may have fit within the structure of early Methodism and whether the hymn would have had different meanings when sung in a society gathering or in a band meeting.

INTRODUCTION TO AFRICAN AMERICAN METHODISTS (40 minutes)

Supplement this section with material from chapters 15 and 17 of Norwood's *The Story of American Methodism*. See also the following web resources: "Recovering the African American Heritage of The United Methodist Church" by Elliott Wright (http://gbgm-umc.org/global_news/full_article.cfm?articleid =5674) and The African American Methodist Heritage Center (http://www.aamhc-umc.org).

Explain that the relationship between white and African American Methodists has mirrored the relational history in the United States. Any and every discussion of this history must deal with the painful matter of slavery. John Wesley wrote "Thoughts upon Slavery" in 1774. (See http://aamhc-umc.org) In this tract, Wesley wrote that "slave-holding is utterly inconsistent with mercy" and further wrote in the tract:

> If, therefore, you have any regard to justice, (to say nothing of mercy, nor the revealed law of God,) render unto all their due. Give liberty to whom liberty is due, that is, to every child of man, to every partaker of human nature. Let none serve you but by his own act and deed, by

> his own voluntary choice. Away with all whips, all chains, all compulsion! Be gentle toward all men; and see that you invariably do unto every one as you would he should do unto you.

Despite this appeal from John Wesley, Methodism in America struggled with racial issues.

Ask for a volunteer to read aloud the section about Richard Allen on pages 13-14 of *Living Our Beliefs: The United Methodist Way*. Invite participants to respond to this section on Methodist history. After a period of group conversation, use the following information to discuss the development of Methodism in the United States:

> The African Methodist Episcopal Church (AME) was the first independent African American denomination. Allen was qualified as a preacher in 1784, at the Baltimore Conference, the first conference of The Methodist Episcopal Church in North America. Allen was ordained by Bishop Francis Asbury and was allowed to lead services at 5 a.m. in 1794. After the action described in *Living Our Beliefs*, Allen organized Bethel AME Church in Philadelphia. He preached and taught and served in mission. In 1816, Richard Allen became bishop of the AME Church. He died in 1831. Among many works, Allen helped to build the Underground Railroad for those escaping slavery in the South.
>
> In 1821, the African Methodist Episcopal Zion Church (AME Zion) was officially formed; however, this church had been in existence earlier. The AME Zion Church traces its history to John Street Methodist Church in New York City. While the church had white and black members, African Americans felt a deep sense of discrimination within the congregation. Members moved out of John Street Church and formed the Zion Chapel of the African Methodist Episcopal Church in 1801. This church became known as Mother Zion Church.

Ask participants if they are aware of AME or AME Zion congregations in their area. If congregations of either denomination are within the experience of class participants, ask them what they know about these denominations.

American Methodism continued to deal with slavery in a manner similar to that of the larger country. Bishop Thomas Coke opposed slavery and his life was threatened as a result of that stand. Coke and Francis Asbury sent a petition to George Washington for the emancipation of slaves in Virginia. While the petition was not successful, early Methodism first opposed slavery. Gradually economic conditions modified the church's position on slavery. Eventually the church split along geographic lines at the General Conference of 1844. The Methodist Episcopal Church and The Methodist Episcopal Church South remained separate until 1939. (The Methodist Protestant Church formed in 1830 as a result of disagreements concerning the power of clergy and bishops. The Methodist Protestant Church also merged into The Methodist Church in 1939.)

Invite participants to ask questions concerning this history. Keep in mind that slavery remains a painful part of American history. Be alert to charged emotions and plan to cut off any speeches that either attack or defend a position. You may also ask the participants how the church split reflects the

Wesleyan understanding of sin as discussed in "The Divine Image Distorted," chapter 5, *Living Our Beliefs: The United Methodist Way*.

DISCUSS WESLEY FAMILY TREE (10 minutes)

Invite participants to share what they have learned about their congregation's history. Ask participants the following question: Which branches of Methodism does your congregation represent?

CLOSING WORSHIP (5 minutes)

Invite the group to sing "Jesus, Lover of My Soul" (*UMH*, no. 479). Ask if participants wish to express thanksgivings, joys, and concerns for prayer. Ask a volunteer to pray.

ASSIGNMENT FOR THE NEXT SESSION

Ask participants to read chapters 6 and 7 of *Living Our Beliefs: The United Methodist Way* as part of their preparation for the next session. If copies of *How Great a Flame!* by James C. Logan are available, ask participants to read chapters 1 and 4.

Session Four

All about Grace

Note to the course leader: Prepare the room. For this session you will need *Living Our Beliefs: The United Methodist Way,* copies of *The United Methodist Hymnal*, and *The Story of American Methodism.*

LEARNING GOAL

Participants will explore the Wesleyan understanding of grace and how it became key to the movement. They will also learn about other churches that are part of the Methodist heritage and will grow in their appreciation of innovation as part of Methodist lay ministry.

OPENING WORSHIP (10 minutes)

Welcome the participants and invite them to sing "And Are We Yet Alive" (*UMH*, no. 553). Introduce the hymn by telling everyone that this hymn is sung at the opening of annual conferences. The Wesley brothers included the hymn in the 1749 collection, *Hymns and Sacred Poems.* John Wesley began the custom of singing the hymn at annual conference. The hymn celebrates our common heritage and further celebrates the grace of God in our lives since our last gathering. After singing the hymn, invite participants to imagine themselves as eighteenth-century Methodist preachers and then read aloud stanzas 3 and 6 of the hymn. Invite a volunteer to pray for the group.

EXPLORE THE WESLEYAN UNDERSTANDING OF GRACE (30 minutes)

Ask a volunteer to read aloud the first paragraph on page 76 of *Living Our Beliefs: The United Methodist Way* (beginning with the words, "The Methodist movement considered"). Ask how this paragraph connects with the church's current mission statement: "The mission of the church is to make disciples of Jesus Christ for the transformation of the world." Say that the mission of making disciples relies on the grace of God and our understanding of such grace.

Ask participants to name how they understand grace. Remind them that the hymns sung during this course celebrate different facets of God's grace. Read the first two paragraphs on page 77 of *Living Our Beliefs: The United Methodist Way* aloud (beginning with "According to Randy Maddox" and ending with "by grace you have been saved"). Tell the class that Wesley understood grace in three actions:

Prevenient (or preventing) Grace

Justifying (or saving) Grace

Sanctifying Grace

Use the material on pages 78-85 of *Living Our Beliefs: The United Methodist Way* to explain these concepts of grace and their relationship to our life journey. If time permits, ask participants to form groups of three. Ask half of the groups to discuss question 2 on page 86 and the other half to discuss question 3 on the same page. Allow time for the groups to report on their conversations to the entire class.

BREAK (10 minutes)

Allow participants time to stretch.

OTHER DENOMINATIONS THAT FORMED THE UMC (20-30 minutes)

Supplement this information with chapters 9 and 10 from *The Story of American Methodism*. In 1939, The Methodist Episcopal Church, The Methodist Protestant Church, and The Methodist Episcopal Church South merged to become The Methodist Church. The movement toward reuniting began with The Methodist Protestant Church and conversations among the groups had been ongoing for at least ten years.

The United Methodist Church was created on April 23, 1968. The denomination includes this historical statement in *The United Methodist Book of Discipline—2008* (page 9):

> On April 23, 1968, The United Methodist Church was created when Bishop Reuben H. Mueller, representing The Evangelical United Brethren Church, and Bishop Lloyd C. Wicke of The Methodist Church joined hands at the constituting General Conference in Dallas, Texas. With the words, "Lord of the Church, we are united in Thee, in Thy Church, and now

in The United Methodist Church," the new denomination was given birth by two churches that had distinguished histories and influential ministries in various parts of the world.

The Evangelical United Brethren Church goes back with two distinct branches to the eighteenth century. Philip William Otterbein (1726-1813) and Martin Boehm (1725-1812), both German-speaking Americans, preached a message of grace and the practices of holy living. In 1800, their followers organized the Church of the United Brethren in Christ. The United Brethren and the Methodists had much in common, including an understanding of grace, the need for accountability, and the desire to live in holiness of heart. Otterbein participated in the consecration of Francis Asbury as a bishop of the church.

Jacob Albright (1759-1808), a Lutheran farmer in eastern Pennsylvania, experienced a conversion under Methodist preaching and teaching. Albright was licensed to preach as a Methodist and was strongly Wesleyan in his understanding of faith. In his version of field preaching, Albright preached in German to the German-speaking people in eastern Pennsylvania. In 1800, when local Methodist authorities forbade him to preach in German, Albright organized a church. A book of discipline came in 1809. In 1816, the Albright churches became known as The Evangelical Association. Because of similarities in theology and church polity, the Church of the United Brethren in Christ and The Evangelical Association merged in 1946. Ask participants if anyone discovered that their congregations have roots in the United Brethren Church or The Evangelical Association. Ask if anyone can trace their roots back to other Methodist denominations.

AN EIGHTEENTH-CENTURY METHODIST (30 minutes)

This information comes from chapter 1 of *How Great a Flame!* by James C. Logan. Tell the following story to participants:

> James Logan wrote a brief story about Martha Thompson, a convert to Methodist Christianity in the eighteenth century. Martha Thompson was born in Preston, England, in 1731. She was poor, but had learned to read and write and was an apprentice to a tailor. At age nineteen she left Preston and went to London where she worked for a wealthy family. One day while on an errand she passed by a large crowd of people and heard thousands erupt in singing a song. She saw a man who was preaching. He wore the gown of a clergyman of his time and stood on a table, commanding the attention of the crowd.
>
> Martha noticed that the crowd included merchants and thieves, the affluent and the impoverished, friends and enemies—a cross-section of London. The message this man preached: "Ye must be born again."

> Curious at first, Martha then became spellbound. She returned home where her mistress lectured her not to listen to that man.
>
> Martha returned several times to hear the man preach. The little man was, of course, John Wesley. One day after a sermon, the crowd sang a hymn by Isaac Watts, "The Lord Jehovah Reigns," and Martha felt a deep inner peace and joy, which Wesley referred to as "the inner witness of the Spirit." Using the words of Isaac Watts' hymn, Martha continued to praise God. She did so even at the home in which she served. Other servants complained to the mistress of the house. Martha was then admitted to the mental institution at Bedlam. Bedlam Hospital was an infamous place where mentally ill persons were confined and treated to the various experiments of the day. People were neglected and abused. Some patients were chained to a wall or floor. Conditions were never better than wretched and dreadful. Martha Thompson, convert to Christ, was sent to Bedlam for the mental illness of praising God.
>
> John Wesley had tried to preach at Bedlam, but was denied permission to do so. He wrote in his Journal: "I have been forbidden to go to Newgate for fear of making them wicked, and now I am forbidden to go to Bedlam for fear of driving them mad." He sent two doctors to Bedlam, and they were able to secure the release of Martha Thompson. Even in Bedlam, Thompson witnessed to Christ. She returned to Preston where there were no other Methodists. In fact, Methodists were despised in Preston. Thompson found a Methodist class that was six miles away. Every Sunday she walked to the class meeting. By 1759, she had gathered a small class of Methodists in Preston. She invited Wesley to come to Preston and visit the class. He finally visited in 1780 and then came three more times during the next ten years.
>
> Martha Thompson lived to age eighty-nine. She ministered to the poor and sick. She led a Methodist class. She participated in society meetings. As she was dying, her children and grandchildren gathered around her bed to sing her home and they sang the hymn by Isaac Watts that first gave the clarity of Christ to Martha: "The Lord Jehovah Reigns."

James Logan concludes the story of Martha Thompson by saying:

> Martha may not have had the facility with words that Wesley had. She did know profoundly, however, in her inner being, the key words of Wesley's preaching—justification and sanctification. She knew herself to have been pardoned by a Father and a Friend. She knew herself to have been given a new birth in Christ Jesus through the Holy Spirit. She knew the empowering, sanctifying grace through the Holy Spirit. "My Father and My Friend." For Martha this was the essence of the gospel. And this because a young woman once heard by chance—or was it not the prevenient grace of Christ—at Moorfields a slight little man proclaim that very word of grace (*How Great a Flame!* page 22).

After telling the story of Martha Thompson, ask participants what Methodist innovations they noted in the story. Invite the class to discuss the influential factors on Martha's unfolding ministry.

CLOSING WORSHIP (10 minutes)

Ask for a volunteer to lead the group in prayer. Invite participants to share any thanksgivings and joys and concerns they may have. After this time of prayer, join in singing stanzas from two hymns by Isaac Watts: "I'll Praise My Maker While I've Breath" (*UMH*, no. 60), stanza 1, and "Come, We That Love the Lord" (*UMH*, no. 732), stanza 4.

ASSIGNMENT FOR THE NEXT SESSION

Ask participants to read chapters 8-11 of *Living Our Beliefs: The United Methodist Way* for the next session and to bring their Wesley family trees. Tell participants that the class will end with the Wesley Covenant Prayer Service and that you would like volunteers to read portions of the service.

Plan to use portions of the service from *The United Methodist Book of Worship* (no. 288). Create an order of service on which the Invitation and Covenant Prayer are printed. You may use paper orders of worship or project the prayers on a screen. For this setting, the longer prayer is preferred rather than the adaptation in *The United Methodist Hymnal.*

Session Five

Ever the Covenant Renewed

Note to the course leader: You will need copies of *The United Methodist Hymnal*, one copy of *The United Methodist Book of Worship*, and copies of the Covenant Renewal Service you have prepared for this session.

LEARNING GOAL

Participants will understand what Wesley identified as the means of grace and how these disciplines lead to holiness of heart. They will recognize that the Methodist heritage is the basis for current ministry. They will further gain an understanding of the Wesleyan quadrilateral in shaping vision for the future. Finally participants will experience a deeper sense of grace and commitment by participating in the Love Feast Service.

OPENING WORSHIP (5 minutes)

Thank participants for their presence in the class. Ask for a volunteer to begin the session with prayer and then sing together "Jesus, United by Thy Grace" (*UMH*, no. 561).

REVIEW THE WESLEY FAMILY TREE (15 minutes)

Ask participants how well they have completed their Wesley family tree. Ask if they have included side branches with Philip William Otterbein and Martin Boehm, representing the United Brethren in Christ, and Jacob Albright, representing The Evangelical Association. You may show the sample included in the appendix or you may have created a Wesley family tree related to your congregation.

HOLY CONVERSATIONS ABOUT THE MEANS OF GRACE (20 minutes)

Point out to participants that chapter 8 of *Living Our Beliefs: The United Methodist Way* is about the means of grace that John Wesley identified. Wesley listed the following means of grace in the General Rules:

> The public worship of God
>
> The ministry of the Word, either read or expounded
>
> The Lord's Supper
>
> Family and private prayer
>
> Searching the scriptures
>
> Fasting or abstinence

Ask if anyone has difficulty understanding these holy practices. Invite participants to consider the role of society, class, and band in helping the early Methodists live in holiness of heart. Then invite participants to form groups of five. Ask each group to discuss the following questions:

> What is your experience with the means of grace?
>
> How can others help you remain accountable in doing these disciplines or practices?
>
> Do you experience accountability in Sunday school classes or other small groups? If not, how could this happen?

As groups continue in conversation, ask them also to discuss Bishop Carder's first question on page 116. After about fifteen minutes, invite the small groups to report to the entire class the nature of their conversation. What new approaches to accountability did they discover? What practices for accountability might they use in their individual lives and in their churches?

BREAK (10 minutes)

Allow participants time to stretch.

THE METHODIST LEGACY (20 minutes)

Ask a volunteer to read aloud the first paragraph on page 120 of *Living Our Beliefs: The United Methodist Way* (beginning with "Walter Brueggemann"). Invite participants to give their definition of church. Then ask them how John Wesley defined church. Let this conversation be guided by pages 120-130. Point out that Carder writes about certain distinctive emphases of Methodism:

Connectionalism: This is the covenantal relationship that exists among individuals, churches, districts, annual conferences, jurisdictional conferences, and the General Conference. Without connectionalism, we would not be able to engage in the global mission and ministry that we currently have.

Itinerancy: Clergy are assigned to churches by bishops in a ministry that is sent. Wesley at first moved preachers every two years, then on an annual basis. Such movement of clergy is a strategy to maximize mission.

Catholicity: Methodism seeks unity among the people of God.

After a brief conversation around these emphases, invite participants to respond to Carder's first question on page 130, which concerns Methodism as a renewal movement. Be certain that the group addresses how the legacy of Methodism helps or hinders reform today.

THE WESLEYAN QUADRILATERAL (20 minutes)

Ask participants if they recognize the term "Wesleyan quadrilateral." Invite them to explain what this term means and how the different parts of the quadrilateral inform the ways in which they live. (Carder deals with this subject on pages 135-145.) If participants are not familiar with the term, draw a quadrilateral on the chalkboard or newsprint and explain what the four sides stand for:

Scripture: the central importance of the Bible to all our actions

Tradition: the importance of church history

Reason: the importance of the gift of mind and mental ability

Experience: the importance of personal and community experience

Ask participants to form four groups. Assign each group one of Carder's questions concerning the aspects of the quadrilateral and have the group respond to these questions. Allow time for each group to report to the entire class.

COVENANT RENEWAL SERVICE (30 minutes)

Invite participants to join in a modified form of the Covenant Renewal service (no. 288 in *The United Methodist Book of Worship*). Use the following order:

Opening Hymn: "Come, Let Us Use the Grace Divine" (*UMH*, no. 606)

Opening Prayer

Scripture Lesson (from those suggested in *The United Methodist Book of Worship*)

Proclamation (*The United Methodist Book of Worship*)

Wesleyan Covenant Service

Invitation

Covenant Prayer (you may use the shorter "Covenant Prayer in the Wesleyan Tradition," *UMH*, no. 607)

Close by singing the first stanza of "Jesus, United by Thy Grace" (*UMH*, no. 561)

Closing Prayer (*The United Methodist Book of Worship*, no. 567)

Appendix

What do you know about United Methodist heritage?

1. Bortnagle Kudzu said, "The only difference between the Methodist church and the Baptists down the street is that they sing different hymns." Is Bortnagle's statement true or false? Why?
2. John Wesley and Jonathan Edwards were both born in 1703. What did they have in common?
3. True or false: Charles Wesley wrote more than seven thousand poems.
4. Aldersgate is significant because it
   a) was a church that began the split that created The Methodist Protestant Church.
   b) is the name of a town where Charles Wesley was inspired to write "O For a Thousand Tongues to Sing."
   c) is a street in London where Methodists preached and prayed.
   d) is the way people summarize John Wesley's experience of grace.
   e) is the name of a new church initiative.
5. Richard Allen was important to Methodism because he was a founder of the AME Church. What do the initials AME mean? Where did this act happen?
6. What denominations formed The United Methodist Church? When?
7. Which of Charles Wesley's hymns is your favorite?
8. True or false: Methodists believe in anything as long as it promotes the love of God.
9. John Wesley was ordained in which church?
10. Who were the historic figures for whom the Cokesbury bookstores are named?

Answers

1. False. The two churches have different understandings of sacraments, grace, church membership, church government, and more. The hymns are indeed different and teach different theological understandings of topics such as grace, forgiveness, the church, baptism, Holy Communion, the church year, and mission.
2. Both were preachers and theologians. Edwards lived in Massachusetts where he also, like John Wesley, engaged in mission work with Native Americans. Neither succeeded in this portion of ministry. Edwards espoused theological positions that differed significantly from those of Wesley.
3. True. Charles Wesley wrote more than nine thousand poems.
4. d. Aldersgate is a shorthand understanding of Wesley's spiritual breakthrough.
5. The African Methodist Episcopal Church formed in 1794 in Philadelphia after efforts were made to prevent Richard Allen from continuing to kneel in prayer at St. George's Methodist Society.
6. The Evangelical United Brethren Church and the Methodist Church merged in 1968.
7. Enjoy the responses!
8. False. Methodists have specific statements of doctrine.
9. Church of England—at Christ Church Cathedral, Christ Church College, Oxford.
10. Thomas Coke and Francis Asbury. These men were appointed by John Wesley to be the first superintendents of the Methodist movement in the United States. Each eventually received the title of bishop.

Wesley Family Tree

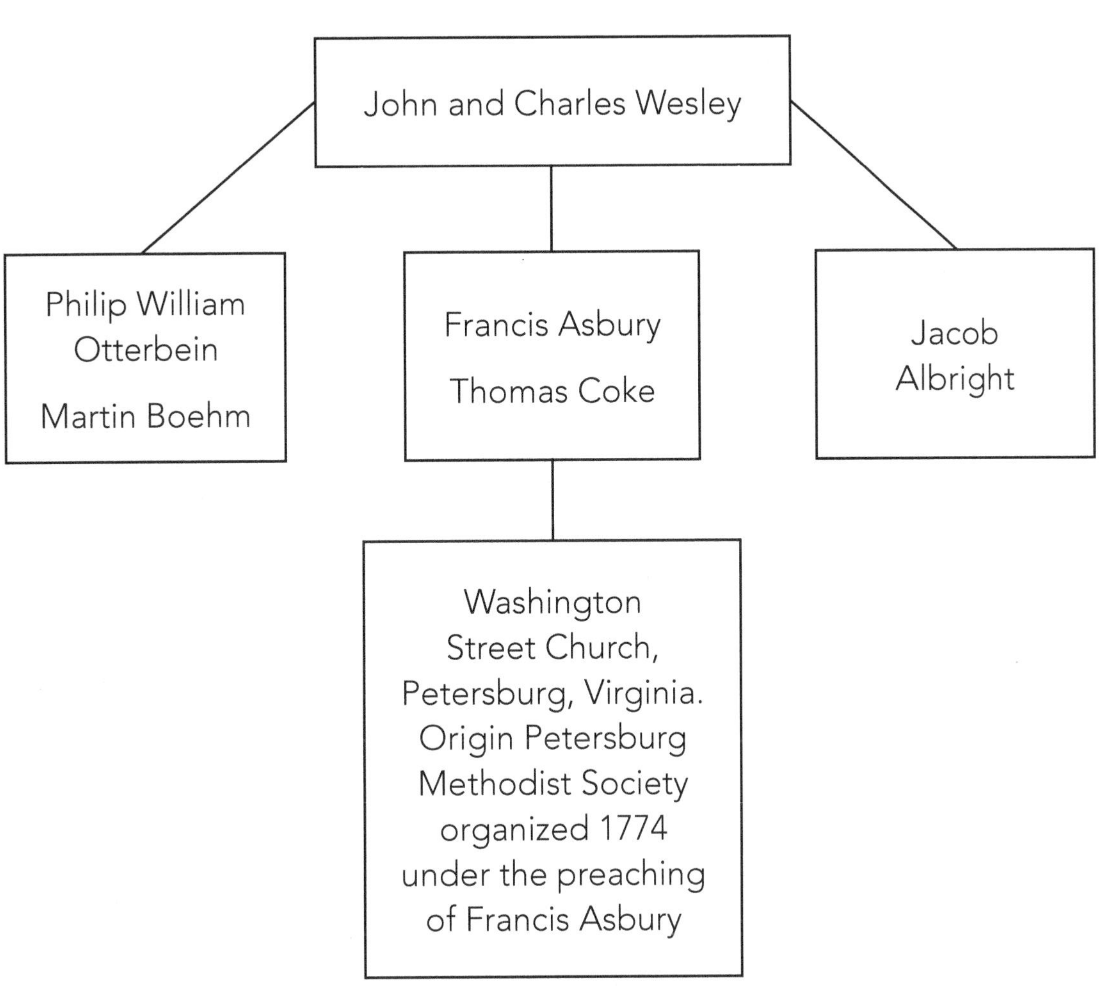

Letter to the Course Participant

An Introduction to Living Our United Methodist Beliefs

When we consider the figure of John Wesley, most often we think of the practical theologian of the eighteenth century. We think of Wesley preaching and teaching around Great Britain, organizing societies and seeking to spread scriptural holiness throughout the land. Such pictures of Wesley fail to help us see the creative genius of Wesley in responding to the needs of the culture surrounding him.

What is most important about this is that our own cultural problems mirror those of Wesley's epoch. As in our time, so in Wesley's time obstacles and barriers grew far more considerably between economic and social classes. The upper class of Wesley's era did little in relation to the poor; those in the Wesleyan societies, who were in a class between England's wealthy and impoverished, related to both rich and poor. Wesleyans of the eighteenth century visited those in debtor's prisons and in mental institutions. By such visits, they helped make visible the caring love of God. In an era in which health care was rare, Wesley wrote *Primitive Physic: An Easy and Natural Method of Curing Most Diseases* as a way to offer rudimentary medical and health education. For more information on such parallels, see *John Wesley for the 21st Century* by John O. Gooch.

Before addressing the social needs as part of his effort to reform the nation, Wesley first began to go to the people. We know about Wesley's field preaching at coalmines and other gathering points. What we fail to remember is that the Church of England did nothing to address these people. The eighteenth-century Anglican church focused primarily on upper class patrons, and the churches were somewhat empty for worship. That moves us to consider a significant parallel with our own era. For many and very different reasons, people are turned off by church. A majority of churches have too many empty seats for worship. To do as Wesley did would mean that we seek creative and new venues for the proclamation of the Gospel. Perhaps this means renting a nightclub for an evening of praise and worship or perhaps it means Bible study groups at the neighborhood coffee house. Perhaps it means offering words of grace on a television commercial during a sports telecast. As we approach the study of our Methodist heritage, I hope that you and your congregation will learn to ask a basic question: What would John Wesley do?

Session Assignments

Session One

The purpose of this session is for participants to learn about the life and ministry of John Wesley. You will gain an awareness of the place of doctrine in the missional movement known as Methodism. You will see the history of Methodism by beginning a Wesley family tree. Before the session, read chapter 1 of *Living Our Beliefs: The United Methodist Way.*

Session Two

The purpose of this session is for participants to gain a deeper sense of John Wesley's theological understanding of God and how that understanding inspired Wesley to create the practical structure and disciplines for the first Methodists. Before the session, read chapters 2 and 3 of *Living Our Beliefs: The United Methodist Way.* Learn more about the start of your congregation and bring your Wesley family tree to the session.

Session Three

The purpose of this session is for participants to be able to identify many of the innovations that came through Wesley and the early Methodist movement. You will also learn about the church's history and the formation of other Methodist denominations. Before the session, read chapters 4 and 5 of *Living Our Beliefs: The United Methodist Way.* Continue gathering information about the start of your congregation and bring your Wesley family tree to the session.

Session Four

The purpose of this session is for participants to explore the Wesleyan understanding of grace and how it became key to the movement. You will learn about other churches that are part of the Methodist heritage and will grow in appreciation of innovation as part of Methodist lay ministry. Before the session, read chapters 6 and 7 of *Living Our Beliefs: The United Methodist Way*. If you have a copy of *How Great a Flame!* read chapters 1 and 4.

Session Five

The purpose of this session is for participants to understand what Wesley identified as the means of grace and how these disciplines lead to holiness of heart. You will recognize that the Methodist heritage is the basis for current ministry and gain an understanding of the Wesleyan quadrilateral in shaping vision for the future. Finally you will experience a deeper sense of grace and commitment by participating in the Love Feast Service. Before the session, read chapters 8-11 of *Living Our Beliefs: The United Methodist Way* and bring your Wesley family tree. The class will end with a Wesley Covenant Prayer Service and volunteers will be asked to read portions of the service.

Session Devotions

Session One

OPENING WORSHIP (15 minutes)

Introduce yourself and allow participants to introduce themselves. After the introductions, sing "And Can It Be that I Should Gain" (*UMH*, no. 363). Use the following information to introduce the hymn, which Charles Wesley wrote after his conversion experience in May 1738: Like his brother John, Charles Wesley struggled to know the love of God and the assurance of forgiveness for himself. In May 1738, Charles recorded the following entries in his journal:

> Wed., May 17th. I experienced the power of Christ rescuing me in temptation. Today I first saw Luther on the Galatians, which Mr. Holland had accidentally lit upon. . . .
>
> Sat., May 20th. I waked much disappointed, and continued all day in great dejection, which the sacrament did not in the least abate. Nevertheless God would not suffer me to doubt the truth of his promises.
>
> [Sunday] May 21, 1738. I now found myself at peace with God, and rejoiced in hope of loving Christ. My temper for the rest of the day was, mistrust of my own great, but before unknown, weakness. I saw that by faith I stood; by the continual support of faith, which kept me from falling, though of myself I am ever sinking into sin. I went to bed still sensible of my own weakness, (I humbly hope to be more and more so,) yet confident of Christ's protection.
>
> [Wednesday] May 24, 1738. At midnight I gave myself up to Christ: assured I was safe, sleeping or waking. I had continued experience of his power to overcome all temptation; and confessed, with joy and surprise, that he was able to do exceedingly abundantly for me, above what I can ask or think.

Both Wesley brothers experienced an assurance of grace as a result of their diligent search and struggle. From that experience, Charles wrote a hymn that he titled "Free Grace," which we know as "And Can It Be that I Should Gain." Let us sing the hymn (or if no musical accompaniment is available, read aloud the words together).

After singing "And Can It Be that I should Gain," ask the group how the hymn connects with their own experience of God's grace. Following a brief time of exchanging stories, invite the group to join in an opening prayer. You may pray the following prayer: Loving God, all-wise and wonderful, to you we give thanks for the beauty of this day and the witness of history. Encourage us to learn about our heritage and to grow in our sense of mission for this time in the life of the world. We join our prayers now together with the words Jesus taught, saying; Our Father, who art in heaven. . . .

CLOSING WORSHIP (5 minutes)

Invite participants to express any prayer requests—joys and concerns—and ask them to join together in prayer. Lead a brief time of prayer and invite participants to join in praying together the Lord's Prayer. After the time of prayer, sing stanzas 3 and 4 of "Come, Sinners, to the Gospel Feast" (*UMH*, no. 339).

Session Two

OPENING WORSHIP (10 minutes)

Invite the class to sing "Maker, in Whom We Live" (*UMH*, no. 88). After singing the hymn, tell the group that John and Charles Wesley taught through their hymns. Ask the class what this hymn teaches about God. You may invite participants to list the specific theological terms in the hymn. Allow time for discussion. Then pray together, thanking God for the class time and for the participants. Invite the presence of the Holy Spirit to sustain and guide the class session.

CLOSING WORSHIP (5 minutes)

Invite participants to join in an affirmation of the Triune God by reciting the Apostles' Creed. Then ask them to express any prayer requests—joys and concerns—and join together in prayer. Lead a brief time of prayer and invite participants to join in praying together the Lord's Prayer.

Session Three

OPENING WORSHIP (10 minutes)

Invite the class to sing "O Come and Dwell in Me" (*UMH*, no. 388). After singing the hymn, tell the group that John and Charles Wesley taught through their hymns. Ask the group to name what they proclaim when they sing "O Come and Dwell in Me." Then pray together, thanking God for the class time and for the participants.

CLOSING WORSHIP (5 minutes)

Invite the group to sing "Jesus, Lover of My Soul" (*UMH*, no. 479). Ask if participants wish to express thanksgivings, joys, and concerns for prayer. Ask a volunteer to pray.

Session Four

OPENING WORSHIP (10 minutes)

Welcome the participants and invite them to sing "And Are We Yet Alive" (*UMH*, no. 553). Introduce the hymn by telling everyone that this hymn is sung at the opening of annual conferences. The Wesley brothers included the hymn in the 1749 collection, *Hymns and Sacred Poems*. John Wesley began the custom of singing the hymn at annual conference. The hymn celebrates our common heritage and further celebrates the grace of God in our lives since our last gathering. After singing the hymn, invite participants to imagine themselves as eighteenth-century Methodist preachers and then read aloud stanzas 3 and 6 of the hymn. Invite a volunteer to pray for the group.

CLOSING WORSHIP (10 minutes)

Ask for a volunteer to lead the group in prayer. Invite participants to share any thanksgivings and joys and concerns they may have. After this time of prayer, join in singing stanzas from two hymns by Isaac Watts: "I'll Praise My Maker While I've Breath" (*UMH*, no. 60), stanza 1, and "Come, We That Love the Lord" (*UMH*, no. 732), stanza 4.

Session Five

OPENING WORSHIP (5 minutes)

Thank participants for their presence in the class. Ask for a volunteer to begin the session with prayer and then sing together "Jesus, United by Thy Grace" (*UMH*, no. 561).

About the Author

George Hovaness Donigian is a United Methodist pastor who has served churches in Virginia and South Carolina. He developed, wrote, and edited Christian education resources for children and then developed books and other resources for all stages of life while working at the General Board of Discipleship in Nashville, Tennessee. He graduated from Berry College and Emory University and participated in the 2007 Oxford Institute of Methodist Theological Studies.

CPSIA information can be obtained
at www.ICGtesting.com
Printed in the USA
LVHW051411090323
740973LV00003B/6